2nd
homonym

SPELLING THROUGH PHONICS
A practical guide for kindergarten through grade three

Marlene J. McCracken

SURREY SCHOOL DISTRICT #36
SURREY, B.C.

AND

Robert A. McCracken

SCHOOL OF EDUCATION
WESTERN WASHINGTON UNIVERSITY
BELLINGHAM, WA

1985

PEGUIS PUBLISHERS LIMITED
520 HARGRAVE ST.
WINNIPEG, MB R3A 0X8

ISBN 0-920541-00-3

First published in 1982 by Marlene J. McCracken
Reprinted 1985, 1986, 1987, 1988 by Peguis Publishers Limited Winnipeg, Manitoba

Printed and bound in Canada

INTRODUCTION

Learning how to spell requires that the child understands how the spelling system works. Although this may seem obvious to the adult, and although many children intuitively come to understand the alphabetic nature of our writing system, many children see spelling as a memorization of letter combinations and make learning to spell an overwhelming task. Further, they never learn the phonics of spelling, and do not generalize nor transfer these learnings to reading. We advocate teaching reading and writing at the same time, beginning both formally in grade one. With this simultaneous teaching, phonics is used in reading with very little direct teaching and the difficulties of rules, long and short vowels, syllabication and the like are obviated.

When teaching this way there is no set sequence, and many children generalize from the alphabetic understandings so that they intuit much of what has not been taught. The spelling taught becomes a sensitive responding to needs as the teacher reads the daily writings of the children.

Marlene J. McCracken
Robert A. McCracken

Surrey, B.C.
October 1982

SPELLING CHECK LIST FOR THE BURLINGTON SCHOOL DISTRICT'S
FOLLOW THROUGH CLASSROOMS

Compiled by: Follow Through Teachers
Washington TRIAD Follow Through
and
Marlene McCracken

This check list is to be used to record a child's independent writing or recording ability. When a child transfers what has been taught in daily dictation to everyday practise, it may be safely assumed that the child has learned what has been taught.

Teachers will keep a file of each child's writing. Independent writing will be collected from each child every two weeks. Approximately four times a year the check lists will be used with the writings. The date will be entered on the appropriate line to indicate when the child has learned each area. Each child need not be judged at the same time. Teachers might do two or three children a week, completing the class in a twelve-week cycle.

Date Learned	KINDERGARTEN "SPELLING" CHECK LIST
_____	Realizes that speech can be recorded in words.
_____	Is beginning to realize what a printed "word" is.
_____	Realizes that words are made up of letters.
_____	Can identify similarities in beginning words.
_____	Can identify similar endings.
_____	Can trace letters and words.
_____	Can copy letters and words.
_____	Can form letters independently.
_____	Can spell and write own first name.
_____	Is beginning to learn the convention of leaving a space between words.

Child's Name _____

_____   Can use _____/m/, _____/f/, _____/t/, _____/s/ and _____/b/
                    correctly in both initial and final positions in a one-syllable
                    word.

_____   Can print correctly a three or four-letter word using the short
                    vowel /a/ and consonants that have been taught.

_____   Can use _____/c/, _____/r/, _____/l/ and _____/p/ correctly in
                    both initial and final positions in a one-syllable word.

_____   Can print correctly a three or four-letter phonetic word using
                    _____ short /o/ and _____ short /a/ and consonants that have
                    been taught.

_____   Can use _____/d/, _____/g/, _____/n/ and _____/w/ correctly in
                    both initial and final positions in a phonetic word.

_____   Can print correctly a three or four-letter phonetic word using
                    _____ short /i/, _____ short /o/ and _____ short /a/ and conso-
                    nants learned.

_____   Can use _____/h/, _____/j/, _____/k/ and _____/v/ correctly in
                    both initial and final positions in a phonetic word.

_____   Can print correctly a four to five-letter phonetic word using
                    _____ short /u/, _____ short /o/, _____ short /i/ and _____ short
                    /a/ and consonants learned.

_____   Can use _____/q/, _____/z/ and _____/y/ correctly in initial
                    positions only.

_____   Is beginning to discern the difference between short /e/ and
                    short /i/.

_____   Can use _____/x/ and /z/ correctly in final positions only.

_____   Can write a one-syllable purely phonetic word correctly.

_____   Can use consonant blends in both initial and final positions.

_____   Can use the word endings of _____/s/, _____/ing/, _____ /y/ and
                    _____/er/ when the root requires no changing.

_____   Can use the digraphs _____sh, _____th and _____ch in initial
                    positions.

_____   Has been introduced to the long vowel sounds and indicates this by
                    spelling _____ long /a/ a-e, _____ long /e/ as e-e, _____ long /i/
                    as i-e, _____ long /o/ as o-e and long /u/ as u-e.

_____   Can write a two-syllable purely phonetic word correctly.

_____   Can use the standard spelling forms of the following words:

_____ the   _____ was   _____ here   _____ one

_____ said   _____ come   _____ saw   _____ you

Child's Name   _____

_____ Uses consonants correctly in both initial and final positions.

_____ Uses consonants in correct sequence.

_____ Can use the _____ short /a/, _____ short /o/ and _____ short /u/ correctly in phonetic words of one syllable.

_____ Is discerning the difference between _____ short /e/ and _____ short /i/ in phonetic words of one syllable.

_____ Can write phonetic words of two syllables using short vowels.

_____ Can add the word endings of ____y, ____s, ____ing, ____ly, ____er, ____ed and ____est to the end of words if the word form does not change.

_____ Can use the consonant digraphs ____ch, ____th and ____sh correctly in both initial and final positions.

_____ Can use the vowel dipthongs ____oi, ____oy, ____ow, ____ou, ____ir, ____er, ____ur, ____ar, ____or, ____ing, ____and, ____ong and ____ung.

_____ Can use correctly the following spelling patterns:

____ck   ____ic   ____er   ____old

____ll   ____ss   ____ff

_____ Indicates knowledge of the generalization that in a two or more syllable word, a short vowel is usually followed by two consonants while a long vowel usually is followed by one consonant.

_____ Can add the word endings ____s, ____ly, ____ed, ____est, ____y, ____ing and ____er when the basic word form changes; i.e., run, running.

_____ Indicates learning of the most common spelling patterns inherent in words with long vowels.

_____ Can discern the long vowel sound and use one of the spelling patterns for that sound:

Long a ____ai, ____a-e, ____ay
Long e ____ee, ____ea, ____e-e, ____ey
Long i ____i-e, ____igh, ____ie, ____y
Long o ____o-e, ____oa, ____ow
Long u ____u-e, ____ew, ____ue

_____ Shows awareness that different ways of spelling the same sound often indicates a change in word meaning.

_____ Has been introduced to and indicates learning in the use of the following contractions:

_____ isn't	_____ he's	_____ can't
_____ won't	_____ he'll	_____ couldn't
_____ aren't	_____ I'll	_____ I'm
_____ wouldn't	_____ don't	_____ she's
_____ she'll	_____ doesn't	

_____ Can spell correctly the common non-phonetic words:

_____ because	_____ the	_____ have
_____ again	_____ is	_____ are
_____ were	_____ was	_____ come
_____ of	_____ saw	_____ said

Child's Name _____

_____ Is able to spell correctly a one-syllable word containing a short vowel sound.

_____ Can use the digraphs _____ch, _____th and _____sh correctly in initial, final and medial positions.

_____ Can use consonant blends in initial, final and medial positions.

_____ Can use the word endings of _____s, _____er, _____ing and _____y when not required to change the basic word form.

_____ Is acquiring skill in correct usage of the long vowel spelling patterns for the following:

Long a _____ai, _____ay, _____a-e, _____eigh
Long e _____ea, _____ee, _____ie, _____e-e
Long i _____i-e, _____igh, _____ie
Long o _____oa, _____o-e, _____ow, _____oe
Long u _____ue, _____u-e, _____ew

_____ Indicates an awareness of "homonyms." Realizes that to change the meaning of a word, one must often change the spelling.

_____ Can write two-syllable or three-syllable words that are totally phonetic.

_____ Indicates awareness that in words containing more than one syllable a short vowel is usually followed by more than one consonant while a long vowel usually has only one consonant following it.

_____ Can correctly add the following word endings to all words:

_____y, _____ing, _____s, _____er, _____est, _____ly

_____ Is acquiring skill in changing word form from singular to plural by adding _____s or _____es, or by changing the y to i and adding es.

_____ Is developing the ability to change word forms from present tense to past tense by adding _____d, _____ed, _____changing the y to i and adding ed.

_____ Is beginning to utilize irregular verb forms.

_____ Can use the vowel digraphs of _____er, _____ar, _____ir, _____ur, _____or, _____oi, _____oy, _____au, _____aw, _____ow, _____ou, _____ short oo, _____ long oo and _____all.

_____   Is developing the ability to spell the common spelling patterns
              of _____ic, _____able, _____tion and _____le.

_____   Is developing the ability to spell and use with meaning the
              prefixes _____re, _____dis, _____un, _____uni, _____bi, _____tri,
              _____be, _____sub, _____super and _____auto.

_____   Spells correctly simple compound words.

_____   Can spell correctly the irregularly patterned words:

              _____ was   _____ the   _____ where
              _____ is   _____ are   _____ there
              _____ one   _____ who   _____ of

_____   Is developing ability in spelling:

              _____ friend   _____ girl   _____ when
              _____ people   _____ does   _____ once
              _____ they   _____ went   _____ their
              _____ because   _____ were   _____ two
              _____ a   _____ right   _____ too
              _____ an   _____ write   _____ off
              _____ tomorrow   _____ said

              Child's Name _____

PHONICS

Phonics is the tool of the writer. Phonics is taught to enable a child
to spell. In order to spell, a child needs to understand three things:

1. The relationship between the sounds of speech and the symbols used to
    record speech sounds. To help children perceive this relationship,
    we first work to establish a child's learning a one-to-one relation-
    ship between the sounds he speaks and the letters he writes. Begin-
    ning learning should be what is easiest for the child. Consonants
    are taught first because one symbol frequently is represented by one
    letter in standard spellings, and because consonants are somewhat
    easier to learn than vowels. Consonants can be felt within the mouth
    because they stop the flow of air. Vowels, whether long or short,
    get lost within the mouth. They cannot be felt and many vowel sounds
    are represented by two or more letters and the same vowel sound may be
    represented by ten or more spellings. For example: day, sleigh, date,
    wait, croquet, cafe, rein or reign, etc.

2. Children need to realize that the symbols that they write should be
    written in the same sequence in which the sounds they represent are
    said. We begin this learning by making the child aware of the sounds
    he says at the beginning of a word, then at the end of a word and
    gradually those in the middle. This is not a strict sequence because
    the child works with discerning the /t/ or the /m/ at the beginning of
    a word, at the end of a word and sometimes in the middle of the word,
    before he works with a second, third or fourth consonant. Nor is /t/
    perfected. It is taught, worked with and practised by the child; then
    we move on to the next sound. Some children need to work with several
    sounds before they are able to discern what is expected; then they often
    learn many at once.

    When the child has learned the one-to-one relationship and the sequencing
    of sounds, he will have grasped the alphabetic principle of our English
    writing system and will be able to spell and write anything he wants to
    say. The spelling will not always be standard, correct spelling, but it
    will provide the child with a base on which to build.

3. The third step in learning to spell is the acquisition of spelling pat-
    terns. The English language is besieged with patterns. Most adults
    are still acquiring some of these spelling patterns. Spelling patterns
    should be taught and practised by the child. In all probability, pat-
    terns will need to be introduced and then reviewed for the child through-

out the years of elementary school. We should begin with the simplest and most commonly used patterns and gradually proceed to the more difficult and rarely used. There is no one sequence. We try to teach those patterns which are obviously missing from a child's writing.

A DIRECTION OF TEACHING PHONICS

KINDERGARTEN

Kindergarten children need to be filled with language, the totality of language. They need to hear the fine language of good literature, they need to hear standard speech patterns and begin to use those patterns to describe their understanding of the world. They need to be filled with the various story patterns of the English language, to re-tell these stories in their own words, to dramatize their understanding of these stories and to illustrate them in many different ways. Kindergarten children need to sing and chant everyday. They need to HEAR language, SEE language and USE language. We believe that a child comes to the act of reading with much more joy, ease and success when the teacher has spent his kindergarten time filling him with language and allowing or encouraging him to use that language in as many ways as possible. Kindergarten children need to gain an understanding of the similarities and differences between the spoken word and the printed word. There are two basic areas of understanding here:

1. Children need to be aware that written English is broken into words. This is very different from spoken language that is not broken between words. Many children, when beginning to learn to write, show that they have not grasped this English writing convention as they join all their written words together in a stream of sounds that resembles speech. Children need much practise in discerning "what a word is." Children confuse words, syllables and common sayings. For example, "How are you" is often identified by children as one word, while "Hallowe'en" will be labeled three words.

2. Young children need to work with similarities in words. They need much practise in recognizing that some words begin the same or end the same. Children need to repeat words after the teacher to help them to "feel" similarities in beginning or ending sounds. A child

has to learn to spell his own speech and so we encourage children to "say" sounds, rather than "hear" sounds.

GRADE ONE THROUGH THREE SEQUENCE

--the sequence of teaching spelling and a suggested procedure throughout the early years.

We consider phonics a spelling skill used when writing, so we begin phonics by beginning spelling and writing. We teach the children five or six consonants. Simultaneously we teach:

1. the name of the letter,

2. the sound the letter represents,

3. the way the letter is written,

4. the way the phoneme is made within the mouth, the way it feels.

We have taught m, b, f, s and t successfully as the first five. These consonants are used frequently and they are made quite differently within the mouth. Except for these two guides, the selection is arbitrary.

> (It should be mentioned that we can discern no "right" way to teach phonics; there seems to be no one right way. We are aware of the incorrectness of isolating consonant sounds. We are aware that it cannot be done but we are also aware of the dangers of not doing so and the problems encountered if all consonant sounds are combined with vowel sounds in order to maintain correctness. The isolation of a sound in the beginning teaching is a momentary device to get children to hear and feel the consonants within spoken language. The sounds are used immediately within words and are practised thereafter as parts of words that a child is writing in a message.)

The children are provided with small chalkboards, approximately 12" x 18", on which they learn to write the letter as they say its name and its sound. This is the first step in teaching the alphabetic principle and the first step in developing the skill of spelling, getting children to understand that if they hear or feel a sound when they say a word that the sound is represented by a letter. Initially a one-sound one-letter relationship is maintained to make it easy for the child to sense the nature of alphabetic spelling.

The second step in the skill of spelling is developing the understanding that spelling requires the sequencing of the sounds within a word. To begin this skill the teacher has the children draw two short lines on their chalkboards:

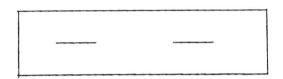

The teacher dictates a word. THE CHILDREN REPEAT THE WORD. The children must learn to spell their own speech; therefore, the teacher must say each word only once for children. Each word that the teacher dictates either begins or ends with an /m'. (We use the slashes to indicate the sound represented by the letter m.) The children are taught to write m in the first space if they feel or hear an /m/ at the beginning or to write an m in the last space if they feel an /m/ at the end. The teacher dictates 8 to 10 words on the first day, 8 to 10 different words on the second day and 8 to 10 different words on the third day. The teacher may hold up pictures, ask the children to identify the picture and to determine if they hear /m/. This entirely eliminates the teacher's saying of the word.

Each new letter is developed in the same way but as new sounds are added, both the old and the new sounds are practised daily on the chalkboards. The teacher will usually dictate monosyllabic words but a sprinkling of polysyllabic words begins the notion that children can spell big words, too, and begins the notion that big words are no harder to spell than little words. Once the teacher has introduced five consonants, a matter of two to four weeks, all five consonants are practised every day by dictating such words as boat, seem, foam, might, surf, moss, team and fib. Once children have the two line notion

11

and the beginning and ending concept fairly well learned, the teacher eliminates the two lines and challenges the pupils to listen for /m/, /b/, /f/, /s/ or /t/ in words like stab, blast, fast, staff, stuff, bats, bets, must, muffs, etc., having the children write three letters in sequence. The teacher should not be surprised if a few children begin to add correct letters such as the l in blast that have not been taught. Children do this once they have discerned the alphabetic principle and the fact that most letters have their sounds within their names. In doing this combined dictation children are practising and reviewing all the letters that have been taught and are thereby learning the sound-symbol relationships and the sequencing of letter sounds.

The adding of a vowel cannot be postponed much longer so we teach short a in initial position following the same steps used for teaching a consonant, except that short /a/ does not exist in final position. We dictate am, at, ask, aspirin, etc. We move almost immediately into medial position and dictate many monosyllabic words which they can now write completely: fat, bat, sat, tat, mat, Sam, tam, fast, mast, aft, stab and words like staff in which the child spells staf. Consonant blends are not mentioned as blends; they are merely taught as sound-sequences. We find that children handle them quite naturally if the teacher says a word once, has the children repeat the word and then asks the children what sound they feel first, what next, what next. If the child writes sb when trying to write stab, he is merely told that he left something out of the middle and that he should say it again and listen. If he writes sab, he is told he left something out, etc. If he writes satb, he is told that he has the right letters but that something is out of order and he is led to correct his sequencing. An integral part of teaching spelling is the correcting of mistakes as they occur so that mistakes are not practised.

With the introduction of the first short vowel, the children's writing on the chalkboards takes on a different form. The children are taught to roughly bisect their chalkboards into four equal-rectangles with their chalk:

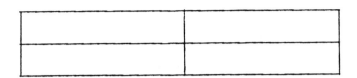

The teacher dictates four words, saying each word once and making sure that the child has recorded the word as correctly as can be demanded. To erase the words, one child is asked to read one of the words and all the children find the word on their chalkboards and erase it; then a second child reads one of the remaining three words orally and all erase it, etc., so that children get practise in writing, spelling and finally word identification.

Additional consonants and short vowels are added in the same way. Long vowels are introduced differently and treated as spelling patterns. The teaching of spelling is described in this paper as a somewhat isolated subject. However, spelling is a skill for writing as a part of a communication program in which children are expected to write at least one message every day. Children are expected to write as independently as possible.

Use Chalkboards.

Allow children to practise
letter formation and sequence
of sounds.

To practise "M", children say the

following words after the teacher, then write

an "m" on their chalkboard in initial or final

position. Teacher dictates eight words every

day.

M

monster	tram	Milwaukee	minimum	macadam
doom	million	material	magnificent	mighty
alarm	ham	inform	mellow	telegram
strum	meat	clam	mom	multiply
mystery	form	stem	harm	macrame
minute	motor	Maggie	Madam	drum
trim	middle	charm	museum	many
mountain	music	market	melody	medicine

S

seven	sunshine	atlas	sorting	sunsets
Sam	bus	support	bakes	seasons
class	San Diego	second	sifter	stops
cress	dress	sixteen	seventy	sports
senior	sunbeam	lakes	Christmas	socks
gets	senior	summer	units	stocking
smooth	sudden	cakes	splinter	sweets
sofa	fuss	sister	spatter	sis

M and S

Sam	sunbeam	stem	mountains
miss	miles	movies	marvelous
slam	mugs	slim	mules
Salem	slum	muss	steam
mandates	scram	millions	storm
mess	surpass	seem	scream
stream	members	markets	solarium
moss	moles	seam	monsters

F

frontier	frown	calf	stiff	off
half	faster	funny	folder	fling
father	belief	reef	beef	if
fifty	further	elf	surf	factory
cuff	off	forest	huff	grief
loaf	deaf	puff	finger	fence
find	freeway	five	friendly	relief
turf	France	leaf	shelf	folder

15

M, S and F

flakes	stuff	flutters	freaks	mutters
muss	form	mischief	molasses	fastens
myself	ferns	firm	storm	midwife
self	fills	matters	scream	fastens
farm	scuff	from	Morris	fosters
farmers	foam	mastiff	serious	masters
muff	furs	flags	matters	fathers
surf	staff	stream	scrams	mothers

B

bleach	butterfly	crab	drab	bathtub
scrub	bacon	cub	beetle	barb
cob	tub	business	stub	bulb
brook	crib	billiard	blotter	Bob
jab	biscuit	glib	grub	blurb
beacon	better	nab	blister	bib
lab	job	bear	knob	basket
boiling	nib	black	butter	mob

M, S, T and B

buff	fob	brim	bits	Bellingham
bass	stiff	firm	stab	bluff
stub	fib	bedlam	biform	broom
sob	mob	boss	biff	blossom
scrub	beef	famous	blab	boom
bakes	beam	fabulous	swab	breaks
mist	blob	bilious	billions	brief
belief	bloom	baffles	Birmingham	bottom

16

T

righ<u>t</u>	limi<u>t</u>	<u>t</u>oday	<u>t</u>able	<u>t</u>en<u>t</u>
<u>t</u>ender	jacke<u>t</u>	headligh<u>t</u>	cos<u>t</u>	<u>t</u>alles<u>t</u>
cu<u>t</u>	<u>t</u>own	par<u>t</u>	<u>t</u>ennis	<u>t</u>igh<u>t</u>
<u>t</u>errible	<u>t</u>ravel	<u>t</u>ired	dentis<u>t</u>	<u>t</u>in<u>t</u>
<u>t</u>errify	sui<u>t</u>	canno<u>t</u>	<u>t</u>rain	<u>t</u>ruan<u>t</u>
cas<u>t</u>	<u>t</u>alking	<u>t</u>erminal	las<u>t</u>	<u>t</u>arge<u>t</u>
<u>t</u>rucking	qui<u>t</u>	buil<u>t</u>	<u>t</u>ooth	<u>t</u>ro<u>t</u>
dar<u>t</u>	<u>t</u>elling	<u>t</u>old	<u>t</u>rouble	<u>t</u>enan<u>t</u>

. . . .

M, S, F, B and T

<u>s</u>kir<u>t</u>	<u>m</u>arke<u>t</u>	<u>t</u>er<u>m</u>	<u>s</u>ummi<u>t</u>	<u>t</u>ennis
<u>f</u>ores<u>t</u>	<u>b</u>u<u>t</u>	<u>s</u>por<u>t</u>	<u>f</u>or<u>t</u>	<u>m</u>is<u>t</u>
<u>t</u>ur<u>f</u>	<u>s</u>i<u>t</u>	<u>f</u>lashligh<u>t</u>	<u>s</u>tar<u>t</u>	<u>f</u>reigh<u>t</u>
<u>b</u>es<u>t</u>	<u>s</u>ea<u>t</u>	<u>s</u>piri<u>t</u>	<u>t</u>u<u>b</u>	<u>s</u>ecre<u>t</u>
<u>s</u>ta<u>b</u>	<u>t</u>ea<u>m</u>	<u>f</u>as<u>t</u>	<u>f</u>i<u>t</u>	<u>f</u>orge<u>t</u>
<u>f</u>a<u>t</u>	<u>s</u>u<u>b</u>	<u>b</u>a<u>t</u>	<u>s</u>a<u>t</u>	<u>f</u>la<u>t</u>
<u>s</u>mar<u>t</u>	<u>s</u>tu<u>b</u>	<u>f</u>as<u>t</u>	<u>f</u>lir<u>t</u>	<u>b</u>ras<u>s</u>
<u>s</u>or<u>t</u>	<u>m</u>ois<u>t</u>	<u>s</u>ur<u>f</u>	<u>b</u>ea<u>t</u>	<u>b</u>ron<u>t</u>o<u>s</u>auru<u>s</u>

. . . .

C

plasti<u>c</u>	<u>c</u>apable	<u>c</u>asual	arithmeti<u>c</u>	<u>c</u>austi<u>c</u>
<u>c</u>lothing	Atlanti<u>c</u>	<u>c</u>oming	<u>c</u>omb	<u>c</u>lassi<u>c</u>
Ar<u>c</u>tic	<u>c</u>omb	<u>c</u>limb	<u>c</u>ompany	<u>c</u>onductor
<u>c</u>olumbine	atti<u>c</u>	giganti<u>c</u>	elasti<u>c</u>	intrinsi<u>c</u>
<u>c</u>urly	<u>c</u>rushing	rusti<u>c</u>	<u>c</u>omplete	<u>c</u>ursive
Pacifi<u>c</u>	anemi<u>c</u>	<u>c</u>reature	drasti<u>c</u>	<u>c</u>lean
<u>c</u>anning	<u>c</u>lass	hecti<u>c</u>	<u>c</u>andy	havo<u>c</u>
publi<u>c</u>	<u>c</u>rush	Antar<u>c</u>tic	dynami<u>c</u>	<u>c</u>ream

17

M, T, F, S, B and C

calf	sporadic	cream	boost	fantastic	cross
mosaic	mystic	float	specific	cat	fabric
socket	class	mosaic	cuff	static	buff
crab	frantic	fleet	Titanic	scarf	film
carnivals	tonic	best	futuristic	coons	fright
cram	can't	cast	clam	botanic	bright
basic	sub	Baltic	talc	Satanic	correct
curb	cut	spoof	calm	Bantam	contrast

. . . .

FURTHER PRACTICE

bionic	cream	mosaic	contest	tablet
crest	fault	classic	bucket	cob
meat	stiff	mindless	clam	first
bathroom	conduct	tyranosaurus	mysterious	boom
settlement	torment	currant	float	cast
beam	Baltic	most	confess	comfort
cobweb	carrot	must	segment	movement
saint	bonnet	mystic	smart	class
fragrant	cliff	cuff	crab	bracelet
bolt	firm	bronotosaurus		

18

ADD A SHORT VOWEL TO YOUR DICTATION

N.B.   Individual enunciations vary, particularly in the vowel sounds. Allow children to learn to spell their own speech.

In order to retain the one-sound, one-letter relationship for beginning children, short vowels rather than long are used.

Short /a/ can be used at the beginning of words. Have children repeat the following words after you. If they say /a/ at the beginning, they print an /a/ in the square on their chalkboard. If they don't say an /a/, they print nothing. Or they MAY print the letter the word DOES begin with if they know it.

DICTATE THE FOLLOWING WORDS AFTER YOU HAVE TAUGHT THE SOUND OF /a/

animal	spend	late	afloat
after	Atlantic	accord	arrange
boil	Alex	and	again
mustard	yellow	aflame	antic
agitate	antelope	monster	crunch
aster	sixth	afford	waist
terrible	absurd	ask	apple
form	tenth	warm	formal

N.B.   /a/ CANNOT BE DICTATED IN A FINAL POSITION AT THIS TIME.   IN THE FINAL POSITION /a/ IS USUALLY A SCHWA AS IN ANNA and AFRICA

DICTATE THE FOLLOWING SET OF WORDS AND CHILDREN WRITE WHAT THEY SAY IN BOTH INITIAL AND FINAL POSITIONS

apricot	acrobat	absorb	aloof
alps	arab	atom	afloat
ant	assault	aft	agleam
apart	alarm	aloft	alert

PLACING /a/ IN A MEDIAL POSITION

N.B. In dictating to children, it is very important that the teacher learns to say the dictated word only once. The children repeat the word as many times as they need to in order to spell the word in correct sequence.

Here are suggestions for

BEGINNING TO DICTATE ENTIRE WORDS

1. The teacher says the word.../fat/

2. Children repeat the word.../fat/

3. Teacher asks, "What did you say first?"

4. Children say /f/ and are instructed to print the letter on the chalkboard.

5. Teacher instructs, "Say /fat/ again."

6. Children repeat word /fat/

7. Teacher asks, "What did you say after the /f/?"

8. Children say /a/ and are instructed to print the /a/ after the /f/ on the chalkboard..."fa"

9. Teacher instructs, "Say /fat/ again."

10. Children repeat word /fat/.

11. Teacher asks, "What did you say after the /a/?"

12. Children respond /t/ and are instructed to print /t/ after the /a/ on their chalkboards..."fat"

CONTINUE IN LIKE MANNER WITH THE FOLLOWING WORDS

tab	am	mast
fat	Sam	bats
bat	fab	mats
mat	tam	tams
sat	stab	tabs
at	fast	stabs

INTRODUCE /r/. CHILDREN PRINT /r/ IN EITHER INITIAL OR FINAL POSITION

robin	reading	war	radar
dear	ripe	lower	rarer
round	ride	rash	roper
pear	raisin	rug	roar
roping	air	shower	roll
liar	power	jar	royal
rodeo	car	really	poor
queer	door	rainy	wear

. . . .

N.B.   In initiating the dictation of entire words, it is necessary to say the word more than once. As soon as the child understands that he must say the word many times, then teacher only says the word once.

/r/ with m, f, s, b, t and c. Children print initial and final sounds

tear	rim	right	repeat
rib	for	roam	sour
roof	stair	flower	rub
rum	redness	relief	moor
bear	riot	clear	root
rot	mirror	roundness	bower
fir	floor	fair	**ram
rob	fear	car	**rat

**   Children print entire word.

. . . .

INTRODUCE /1/...CHILDREN DECIDE WHETHER THE DICTATED WORD BEGINS OR ENDS WITH /1/

land	peal	well	listen	wall	leash	veil
pal	goal	leg	lead	heal	pail	entail
gill	load	log	deal	long	shell	lower
pill	jail	dial	natural	doll	latch	leap

<u>/l/</u> with m, f, s, b, t, c and r. Children print the initial and final sounds.

<u>liar</u>	<u>frail</u>	<u>lift</u>	<u>lost</u>
<u>real</u>	<u>tell</u>	<u>let</u>	<u>fool</u>
<u>leaf</u>	<u>loam</u>	<u>coal</u>	spool
<u>soul</u>	<u>light</u>	<u>sail</u>	<u>cowl</u>
<u>steal</u>	<u>till</u>	<u>ball</u>	towel
<u>feel</u>	<u>sell</u>	<u>sill</u>	<u>lot</u>
<u>bell</u>	<u>meal</u>	<u>fowl</u>	<u>tool</u>
<u>lab</u>	<u>royal</u>	<u>call</u>	<u>real</u>

. . . .

<u>m, f, s, b, t, c, r or l.....with /a/.</u> Children print entire word.

slat	scram	flat	tram	lam	lasts
slam	clam	slab	last	slabs	flats
cram	crab	<u>flam</u>	lab	slats	slams

. . . .

INTRODUCE /p/. CHILDREN DECIDE WHETHER THE DICTATED WORD BEGINS OR ENDS WITH /p/

deep	grip	plod	personality
pig	prison	drip	yelp
gallop	dip	dump	heap
nap	pretty	grasp	chimp
peeking	plug	hoop	prod
weep	thump	cheap	plop
pried	poking	person	peep
probably	pride	shrimp	help

. . . .

m, s, f, t, c, b, r, 1 and p. Children print both initial and final letter.

peas	bump	coop	post
peat	flap	fantastic	reap
top	panic	peril	slump
sloop	petal	possum	plier
loop	creep	tip	poet
pool	perfect	lump	pear
stop	pail	flop	proof
bottom	poem	pram	prop

N.B.   IT SHOULD BE NOTED AT THIS TIME THAT MANY CHILDREN WILL WANT TO PRINT MORE
THAN THE BEGINNING AND ENDING SOUNDS.   THEY WILL WANT TO PRINT ALL THE LETTERS
THEY KNOW IN EACH DICTATED WORD.   THIS SHOULD BE ENCOURAGED.   IT HELPS TO
DEVELOP "SEQUENCE OF SOUNDS."   e.g. in "stop"...the child might print "st..p"
or in "petal"...the child might print "p..t..l"

m, s, f, t, c, r, 1, p and /a/. Children print the entire word.

past	flap	trap	lamp
cap	rap	spat	camp
tap	slap	flap	stamp
pat	clamp	slaps	clasp
lap	fact	pram	pact
strap	laps	rasp	pats
pals	map	maps	taps
clap	**part**	caps	claps

INTRODUCE SHORT VOWEL "O"

AFTER TEACHING THE SOUND OF SHORT /o/ TO CHILDREN, DICTATE THE FOLLOWING

WORDS. CHILDREN WRITE THE BEGINNING AND ENDING SOUNDS.

octopus	off	optimum
object	observant	oddness
odds	omnibus	osmosis
offset	operator	otter

. . . .

NOW DICTATE /o/ IN A MEDIAL POSITION IN THE SAME MANNER AS YOU INTRODUCED /a/

IN A MEDIAL POSITION. CHILDREN SPELL THE ENTIRE WORD.

pot	sob	fob	soft
lot	slob	stop	loft
rot	mop	plop	croft
cop	flop	prop	cops
cot	tops	spot	lots
top	Bob	clot	blots
rob	cob	blot	crops
slot	trot	plot	stops

. . . .

INTRODUCE THE CONSONANT /d/. CHILDREN WRITE INITIAL AND FINAL LETTERS.

doom	lard	mold	send
deal	mid	dramatic	mood
dead	drat	road	dust
dart	told	drop	find
fund	read	card	mend
bald	bold	bend	tried
drastic	damp	dear	dries
cold	lend	food	tend

/d/ WITH VOWELS /a/ AND /o/. CHILDREN WRITE ENTIRE WORD.

pop	mad	dam	cost
dot	bad	dad	cast
drop	sad	clad	cot
cod	cad	scads	cat
pod	pad	sod	mop
plod	fad	plods	map
lap	lad	pads	clod
dots	slap	dabs	cads

. . . .

INTRODUCE THE CONSONANT /g/. CHILDREN WRITE BEGINNING AND ENDING LETTERS.

gravel	slub	mug	gob
rug	bug	gull	gust
fog	grog	gram	gill
cog	flag	gleam	gut
fold	big	grab	grass
flog	pig	brag	great
gulf	fig	gear	gallon
gum	grasp	peg	grip

. . . .

USING /g/ WITH /a/ AND /o/. CHILDREN SPELL THE ENTIRE WORD.

bag	stag	gab	stags
gas	gap	gasp	flags
tag	gag	slag	gags
gal	flag	bags	grabs
bog	dog	log	flogs
got	fog	smog	agog
cog	cogs	togs	grog
golf	clog	frog	dogs

25

REVIEW OF ALL LETTERS LEARNED SO FAR. CHILDREN WRITE THE ENTIRE WORD.

scat	frost	romp	bag
smog	cost	ramp	bog
crop	pots	lost	sag
atop	soft	last	sog
mad	pact	flag	pram
damp	fact	flog	prom
lamp	tact	tap	cram
tramp	past	top	gram

. . . .

WITH CHILDREN WHO HAVE BEEN USING FRAME SENTENCES, A SHORT SENTENCE COULD BE
DICTATED EVERY OTHER DAY. CHILDREN WILL PRACTICE THE COMMON WORDS USED AND
BECOME AWARE OF CAPITAL LETTERS AND PERIODS.

e.g. I have a dog.	I like a frog.
I see the frost.	I see a cat.
My cat is mad.	I can golf.

. . . .

INTRODUCE THE CONSONANT /n/. CHILDREN PRINT THE INITIAL AND FINAL LETTERS.

news	seen	tin	torn
nabob	men	fun	corn
green	ten	sun	born
near	neat	ton	teen
begin	sin	fin	plain
fallen	nib	net	sewn
nest	bun	spin	blown
been	darn	mean	coin

REVIEW OF ALL LETTERS.   CHILDREN WRITE THE ENTIRE WORD.

plan	can	stand	sand
ban	fan	snap	land
fan	man	snag	gland
not	ant	pond	plant
nod	Stan	fond	slant
pan	not	bond	clan
nap	nob	nag	plan
nab	snob	band	ran

. . . .

INTRODUCE THE CONSONANT /w/.   CHILDREN PRINT INITIAL AND FINAL LETTER.

warm	waist	wagon
waif	war	wool
west	warp	wood
wafer	worm	wig
wait	word	wag
was	worst	woolen
want	wart	wolf
wind	wand	wail

. . . .

INTRODUCE THE SHORT VOWEL /i/ SOUND.   THEN DICTATE THE FOLLOWING WORDS.   CHIL-
DREN PRINT THE BEGINNING AND ENDING LETTERS.

Indian	imagination	illustration	inbred
idiot	impart	impress	impair
import	indeed	important	indent
illegal	independent	impersonal	inboard
immortal	imperial	incur	imprint

SHORT /i/ WITH m, f, t, s, b, c, r, 1, p, d, g, n AND w.   CHILDREN PRINT THE
ENTIRE WORD.

fit	spit	snip	tilt
wig	win	swim	silt
sit	flit	sift	lilt
big	slit	swift	gilt
wit	wind	gift	slip
dig	spin	lift	slim
pit	flip	mist	slid
bit	clip	fist	strip

. . . .

REVIEW OF ALL LETTERS TAUGHT SO FAR.   CHILDREN PRINT ENTIRE WORD.

fast	drop	flit	sift
fist	drip	flat	soft
sip	slip	mist	crisp
sap	slap	mast	wisp
grin	clip	cost	spot
grand	clop	list	spit
trip	limp	lost	mint
trap	lamp	last	lint

. . . .

INTRODUCE /h/.   CHILDREN PRINT INITIAL AND FINAL LETTERS.

hear	Helen	hurt	hurl
hoard	heap	held	havoc
humor	half	hug	Harold
help	horn	heel	hamster
hostess	homer	harp	heart
helmet	heron	hippopotamus	homeward

/h/ WITH VOWELS /a/, /o/ AND /i/. CHILDREN PRINT THE ENTIRE WORD.

hop	hand	has
had	hog	hip
hid	hag	hilt
hit	ham	hint
hat	him	hasp
hot	his	hats

INTRODUCE THE CONSONANT /j/. CHILDREN PRINT AT LEAST THE BEGINNING AND ENDING LETTERS.

joker	jasmin	jaguar	jackpot
jackal	journal	just	jester
jail	jacket	John	jar
jeer	James	Japan	jewel
jump	joint	jargon	jurist
junior	Jerusalem	Jean	Justin

INTRODUCE THE CONSONANT /k/. CHILDREN PRINT AT LEAST THE BEGINNING AND ENDING LETTERS.

kipper	keg	keen
Karen	Kelvin	kept
kennel	keeper	kernel
keep	keel	killer
kerchief	kelp	kindergarten
kid	kindred	kindness
kilt	kinder	kiss
kitten	king	kink

INTRODUCE THE CONSONANT /v/.   CHILDREN PRINT AT LEAST THE BEGINNING AND
ENDING LETTERS.   ENCOURAGE CHILDREN TO ADD MEDIAL SOUNDS.

veil	verbal	veal	veer
vacant	violet	vault	valiant
vacuum	vagabond	vertical	veteran
vain	velvet	vamp	violin
valid	vacation	vagrant	ventriloquist
vapor	Venus	various	volcanic

. . . .

REVIEW /v/, /h/, /k/, /j/ AND /w/ WITH THE KNOWN VOWELS.   CHILDREN WRITE THE
ENTIRE WORD.

jam	vat	van	jag
jog	hilt	vast	job
kilt	king	twin	wig
jilt	jug	twist	wag
wilt	kin	twig	hag
wind	jot	jig	hog

. . . .

INTRODUCE SHORT /u/.   TEACH CHILDREN THE SOUND OF "SHORT /u/", THEN DICTATE
THE FOLLOWING WORDS REQUIRING CHILDREN TO SPELL AT LEAST THE INITIAL AND FINAL
SOUNDS.

under	unravel	unbend	unfair
umpteen	uphill	understand	unbelief
uncoated	unarm	until	unfold
underarm	undecided	upon	underhand
unfed	upper	underleaf	uplift
undercast	underfed	underwear	uproot

REVIEW OF ALL LETTERS LEARNED THUS FAR. CHILDREN SPELL ENTIRE WORD.

(m, f, s, t, b, c, r, l, p, d, g, n, w, h, j, k, v, a, i, o and u.)

bug	dug	clip	spuds
bag	dig	clog	suds
big	dog	clap	glad
bog	rug	stub	strum
hug	rag	stab	strut
hag	rig	swim	slam
hog	hut	swam	slum
brag	hot	swum	slim

MORE REVIEW WITH ALL LETTERS LEARNED SO FAR. CHILDREN WRITE ENTIRE WORD.

(m, f, s, t, b, c, r, l, p, d, g, n, w, h, j, k, v, a, i, o and u.)

just	jump	must	punt
crust	bust	hum	stunt
trust	dust	him	runt
gust	stump	ham	bunt
rust	stamp	hunt	tuft
bump	stomp	hint	skit
skip	dump	spin	slug
skim	lump	spun	smug

INTRODUCE THE CONSONANT /y/. CHILDREN PRINT AT LEAST THE BEGINNING AND ENDING

SOUNDS.

yet	yell	yacht	yak	yam	yap
yard	yank	yarn	yes	year	York
yawl	yearn	yeast	yokel	yawn	yip
yelp	yolk	yield	yo-yo	yonder	yelper

31

<u>INTRODUCE /qu/.   CHILDREN PRINT THE /qu/ AND AT LEAST THE ENDING SOUND</u>

<u>OR THE VOWEL THAT FOLLOWS /qu/.</u>

queen	quill	quell	quad
quilt	quite	quit	quadruped
question	quiet	quarter	quaint
quest	quick	quintuplet	quarrel
quiver	quip	queer	quaver
quail	quartz	quiz	quake

. . . .

<u>INTRODUCE THE CONSONANT /z/.   CHILDREN PRINT AS MUCH OF THE WORD AS THEY</u>

<u>ARE ABLE.</u>

zinc	whiz	jazz	zoo
zip	quiz	razz	zany
zipper	friz	zero	Zuni
zest	buzz	zebra	zing
fizz	fuzz	zeal	zone

. . . .

<u>INTRODUCE THE CONSONANT /x/.   CHILDREN PRINT THE ENTIRE WORD.</u>

N.B.   Children should be aware that /x/ is a letter that is rarely used.
In initial positions, it never has the sound of /x/ (that I know of)
and is rarely used in final position. /cks/ usually takes the place
of /x/.

ox	six	sex
box	fix	vex
pox	nix	tax
fox	mix	wax

TEACH CHILDREN THE SOUND OF THE SHORT VOWEL /e/. THEN DICTATE THE FOLLOWING

WORDS. ALL THE CONSONANTS HAVE BEEN INTRODUCED AND ALL THE VOWELS, SO CHIL-

DREN SHOULD BE ABLE TO WRITE PURELY PHONETIC ONE-SYLLABLE WORDS PERFECTLY.

wet	hem	red	mend
met	stem	bed	send
pet	hen	led	lend
get	den	bled	bend
let	glen	sled	tend
net	Ben	wed	wend
set	pen	fed	spend
bet	ten	fled	blend
west	tent	left	weld
nest	went	cleft	elf
best	sent	deft	self
pest	spent	beg	belt
jest	bent	leg	felt
lest	help	peg	melt
rest	yelp	keg	welt
test	kelp	Ted	held

. . . .

DICTATION OF TOTALLY PHONETIC ONE-SYLLABLE WORDS...TO REVIEW ALL THE LETTERS

TAUGHT AND SEQUENCING SOUNDS

blab	crisp	stop	crab	bump	gun	grab
skid	plop	bled	if	frog	hunt	pig
nod	mint	sad	rug	self	pond	rob
bug	cab	hog	gulp	stab	lump	grunt
web	hid	blond	fled	dig	rim	sift
glad	plug	soft	mad	blob	went	raft

33

belt	kept	twist	crust	print
him	twin	quiz	loft	dad
golf	plod	flint	craft	help
romp	bud	grim	trend	sob
jam	slept	drip	slim	mud
swim	brag	rent	sift	fig
pad	held	sod	run	skin

. . . .

CHILDREN WILL NOW ENJOY WRITING TWO-SYLLABLE PURELY PHONETIC WORDS

STEPS: Teacher says, "cabin," children repeat /cabin/ after the teacher.

Teacher asks children to clap to the word /cabin/.

Children will usually clap twice.

Then children are directed to draw two lines on the chalkboard. (one for each clap)

WRITING PURELY PHONETIC TWO-SYLLABLE WORDS

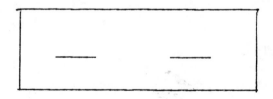

Teacher asks children to repeat /cabin/ clapping again.

Teacher asks, "What did you say on the first clap?"

Children respond, "cab" and are directed to print /cab/ on the first line.

Teacher asks, "What did you say on the next clap?"

Children respond, "in" and are directed to write /in/ on the second line.

Then children are directed to write the entire word /cabin/ underneath.

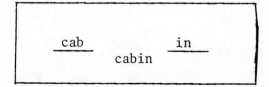

DICTATE THE FOLLOWING LIST FOUR OR FIVE WORDS AT A TIME, IN THE MANNER
DESCRIBED ON THE PREVIOUS PAGE.

humbug	prevent	cabin	replan
nutmeg	inlet	present	upset
husband	invest	repent	motel
intend	control	contest	request
repast	frantic	revolt	depend
insect	unkind	unwind	conflict
defend	instruct	panic	intent
habit	credit	inland	resist
exit	debit	antic	comic
expend	invent	suspect	contest
exact	satin	encamp	cosmic
expand	invest	mishap	April
extent	enact	plastic	oldest
context	react	relax	golden
exist	sedan	hotel	music
exam	protect	pretend	final

. . . .

ADDING THE ENDINGS /s/, /ing/, /y/ AND /er/.

MOST CHILDREN SHOULD FIND ADDING ENDINGS A RELATIVELY SIMPLE TASK. DICTATE
AS MANY WORDS FROM EACH LIST UNTIL CHILDREN ARE COMFORTABLE IN THEIR DICTATION.

ADDING "S"...IN WORDS WHERE THE ROOT REQUIRES NO CHANGE.

dusts	hams	cats	bands
crusts	hens	hands	wilts
runs	pigs	bins	stands
jumps	jams	lists	fits
hops	dogs	taps	mists
skips	buns	sits	tilts

bits	mats	stubs	rugs
bans	spots	beds	bets
steps	cans	bats	jigs
flags	lasts	spits	sags
dents	pots	pins	flats
pans	strums	weds	wigs
wets	brats	bags	bugs
wins	rags	hats	rusts

---

digs	nests	stabs	ponds
mugs	tests	pests	vests
prints	buds	dims	crafts
rests	figs	rents	bumps
plugs	grants	skins	lumps
golfs	rafts	jests	cabs
swims	crests	crabs	skids
twists	twins	drips	hunts

· ·

ADDING /ing/ TO THE END OF A WORD WITHOUT CHANGING THE ROOT.

standing	handing	blinking	sanding
sending	bending	frisking	winking
granting	cresting	tending	acting
jumping	masking	casting	milking
asking	hunting	dusting	tinting
resting	basking	bumping	nesting
blending	tenting	bunting	wending
planting	lasting	welding	stinking

---

jilting	twisting	banding	bunting
mending	minding	hinting	clumping
finding	rusting	jesting	flunking
denting	risking	golfing	slinking
printing	ending	renting	junking
slanting	landing	belting	bunking
misting	testing	melting	sinking
grunting	linking	pelting	pinking

· ·

ADDING /y/ TO THE END OF THE WORD WITHOUT CHANGING THE ROOT.

sandy	spunky	clumsy	jumpy
candy	softy	risky	junky
handy	crusty	pesty	bumpy
rusty	cranky	crispy	grumpy
dusty	lefty	slinky	flunky
misty	frisky	lumpy	milky
nasty	silky	hefty	twisty
gusty	crafty	flinty	dandy

crampy	sulky	testy
clanky	limpy	linty
pinky	springy	stumpy
silty	kinky	stringy
crimpy	windy	clingy
stinky	wispy	stingy
minty	lofty	swingy

37

ADDING /er/ TO THE END OF A WORD WHEN THE ROOT DOES NOT CHANGE

faster	pester	pilfer	helper
sender	boxer	fluster	renter
fender	gander	planter	stricter
buster	filter	plunder	milder
tinder	plaster	ringer	winter
master	milker	sander	stomper
crisper	blister	blaster	golfer
bumper	mender	wilder	duster

---

blunder	finger	sprinter	older
aster	after	stamper	under
camper	singer	springer	fonder
spender	swinger	hinder	bolder
blinder	sister	pelter	yonder
mister	fester	fluster	colder
grander	grinder	tender	stinger
welder	linger	jester	folder

. . . .

INTRODUCING THE DIGRAPH /ch/ IN INITIAL AND FINAL POSITIONS...IN PURELY PHONETIC WORDS.

chest	chub	lunch	much	belch
chat	chant	bunch	bench	branch
chump	chesty	munch	inch	charm
chimp	child	punch	flinch	clinch
champ	chug	crunch	drench	welch
chap	Chester	pinch	ranch	brunch
chip	children	finch	hunch	scrunch

38

INTRODUCING THE DIGRAPH /sh/ IN INITIAL AND FINAL POSITIONS...IN PURELY
PHONETIC WORDS.

shiver	shining	fish	bash
shag	shaft	flash	dish
shed	shop	ash	mash
shanty	shelf	mesh	hush
ship	shoplift	gush	dash
shelter	shot	gash	crush
shut	sham	rush	mush
shunt	shush	sash	rash
swish	hash	splash	lush
wish	smash	lash	brush

. . . .

INTRODUCING THE DIGRAPH /th/ IN INITIAL AND FINAL POSITIONS...IN PURELY
PHONETIC WORDS.

that	theft	both
this	thing	moth
then	thrash	fifth
than	thrift	bath
them	thinly	filth
thunder	thrush	tenth
thump	thresh	math
thin	thundering	sixth
with	cloth	seventh
ninth	path	froth
eleventh	lath	mouth

CH, SH AND TH

CH

chop	children	chimp	chapter	hunch
chip	chicken	chump	pinch	punch
chug	chink	achoo	inch	bunch
chum	chant	drench	French	finch
chap	chest	stench	ranch	porch
charm	much	bench	branch	lunch
champ	such	richly	clinch	crunch
child	rich	clench	belch	enchant

TH

thin	then	gothic	bath	forth
this	throb	northern	math	north
that	thick	bathtub	path	tooth
thus	thank	athlete	ninth	broth
thorn	think	thrash	fifth	cloth
three	thing	pathway	sixth	both
the	these	teething	Beth	smooth

SH

shut	ash	mash	gush	shark
ship	slash	rash	refresh	rasher
shop	cash	sash	splash	flesh
shoo	dash	crush	lush	flushing
short	flash	shunt	flush	slush
shorn	gash	dish	mesh	finish
smash	hash	fish	mush	plush

LONG VOWELS MIGHT BE INTRODUCED TO FIRST GRADE CHILDREN BY INTRODUCING THE SIMPLE SPELLING PATTERN OF VOWEL-CONSONANT-VOWEL FOR EACH LONG VOWEL SOUND.

LONG a

came	mane	gate	take
same	Jane	late	rake
blame	crane	mate	bake
shame	lane	skate	sake
dame	pane	fate	wake
fame	flame	hate	flake
game	tame	plate	shake
lame	name	rate	snake

———————

pale	made	ape	safe
scale	jade	cape	drake
gale	blade	gape	fake
male	shade	grape	quake
sale	wade	shape	stake
stale	bare	tape	awake
dale	dare	drape	plane
bale	fare	escape	vane

. . . .

LONG e

N.B.   THERE ARE VERY FEW WORDS USING LONG /e/ IN THIS SPELLING PATTERN.

these...theme...here...mere...eve...Steve   Pete

. . . .

LONG o

rope	bone	home	drove
hope	hone	dome	cove
cope	cone	rode	dove
slope	prone	code	grove
mope	stone	pole	rove
dope	tone	hole	woke
lope	alone	stole	choke
pope	show	mole	coke

---

probe	chose	yoke	shore
elope	those	broke	sore
mope	hose	joke	spore
grope	close	poke	snore
impose	nose	stroke	yore
unclose	prose	scope	wore
pose	rose	globe	more
sole	arose	robe	store

. . . .

LONG i

hide	hive	file	dine
ride	dive	pile	wine
bide	five	mile	fine
side	chive	tile	brine
slide	jive	vile	shine
wide	live	bite	thine
glide	aside	kite	line
bride	inside	spite	find

chime	vine	fire	wife
slime	lime	wire	life
dime	mime	hire	strife
grime	prime	mire	fife
mine	time	tire	stile
nine	rise	bribe	gripe
pine	arise	jibe	pipe
spine	wise	tribe	smile

. . . .

LONG u

use	crude	fume
fuse	rude	plume
abuse	nude	prune
amuse	cute	dune
muse	duke	tune
tube	fluke	dupe
rube	rule	pure
cube	yule	cure

. . . .

GRADE ONE "DOOZERS"

the	come	said	one
was	have	once	is
of	are	you	

Children should become familiar with these in their daily spelling and learn to spell them correctly.

43

GRADE TWO DICTATION

Begin the year by reviewing the sequence of sounds, consonants and short vowels.

SHORT a

stand	grasp	and	hand
clamp	camp	lamp	had
draft	slant	sand	bat
plant	damp	sad	bad
blast	grant	tramp	flat
ask	flap	blank	fast
brand	band	drank	mast
trash	strap	thank	stamp

---

ham	crab	ash
champ	blab	flash
cramp	stab	crash
ban	drab	brash
can	slab	gash
clan	tab	lash
fan	flam	slash
Dan	jab	smash

. . . .

SHORT e

spend	trend	pest	wet
blend	spend	chest	bet
end	nest	jest	get
bend	west	test	jet
lend	vest	left	let
mend	best	cleft	met

44

tent	wed	fresh	send
went	shed	felt	tend
bent	bled	melt	crest
sent	fed	them	rest
dent	Fred	slept	went
ten	sled	bend	vent
then	step	check	pet
net	tend	red	set

. . . .

SHORT o

slop	chomp	chop	not
flop	lost	hop	cot
cost	drop	clop	got
plop	trod	crop	hot
plod	frost	pond	shot
shot	cost	romp	jot
blot	lost	soft	lot
stop	shop	bond	slot

_____

pop	jog	frog	romp
prop	bog	log	stomp
rot	cog	smog	chomp
tot	clog	fond	pomp
flock	dog	bond	clomp
frock	fog	Fonda	odd
clock	flog	Honda	off
stock	hog	on	mop

45

SHORT i

drift	spit	drip	ink
sift	split	skip	pink
lift	lit	dip	stink
swift	hit	slip	think
shift	bit	trip	drink
fist	fit	clip	slink
list	flit	snip	mink
mist	pit	tip	chink

——————————

wind	lick	slim	thing
twig	brick	thin	swing
lint	trick	in	sling
glint	slick	chin	spring
hint	imp	blimp	fling
mint	limp	chimp	sting
tint	crimp	din	bring
stick	shrimp	fin	king

· ·

SHORT u

hunt	just	drum	lump
bunt	trust	strum	slump
punt	dust	gum	duck
runt	rust	plum	stuck
hut	crust	clump	luck
shut	must	dump	truck
shunt	trust	stump	cluck
blunt	gust	jump	chuck

46

much	shush	gun	bunch
such	mush	slug	punch
gush	plush	hug	lunch
hush	rush	bug	crunch
brush	crush	rug	hunch
flush	sun	tug	munch
slush	fun	plug	dusk
blush	bun	thump	tusk

REVIEW OF THE "SHORT VOWELS"

Teach word endings /er/, /ing/, /y/, /es/, /s/ and /ed/.

SHORT a

plants	blasting	rafter	grander	acting
planter	masts	after	bands	facts
planting	past	draft	casting	tact
sandy	casting	shafts	bath	plans
pansy	vast	grants	math	hams
patsy	lasting	daft	path	ants
handy	nasty	flanks	jams	glands
dandy	pantry	lanky	prams	ramps

―――――――――――

crafty	clasped	clasp	rang	tramped
thanks	gasping	apt	sang	cramping
chanting	raspy	flask	hang	asking
ranking	grasped	masked	clang	basks
tanker	crashing	flashing	slang	crab
pranks	rashes	clashed	bang	flab
pants	trashy	crashed	fang	drab
slanting	cashing	thrash	gang	slab

―――――――――――

landing	camps	bashing	hangs	stabs
stands	camper	dashing	sprang	Brad
hands	camping	lashed	scrams	cranker
plaster	damper	mashing	plans	banker
faster	hamper	sashed	clans	Frank
canter	stamps	splashing	bans	blanks
branding	canoeing	gashed	crams	shank
shanty	lamps	hash	grams	clanking

48

REVIEW OF THE "SHORT VOWELS"

Teach word endings /er/, /ing/, /y/, /es/, /s/ and /ed/.

SHORT e

belted	slender	benches	frenzy	bending
gelding	render	drenching	empty	lends
welded	wending	French	enemy	mending
felt	tents	ending	smelter	sending
melted	renting	vespers	Denver	western
pelting	vending	extra	metal	tender
smelting	zesty	flexing	denting	tending
melding	spending	hexing	petal	westerner

---

rests	fresher	fleshy	medal	entry
jesting	meshing	stench	pedal	twenty
lest	helper	steps	trembling	dented
nesting	shelf	swept	very	spent
pester	elfin	lefty	plenty	rents
testing	Welsh	hefty	tempest	herself
bets	pesky	held	kept	venting
best	desks	vexing	kelp	tenting

---

vests	shelter	deftly	text	hems
creating	presto	swelter	blest	hens
chesty	temper	member	render	Fred
lest	tempting	Dexter	never	weds
trends	fester	detect	trends	then
blender	depths	inject	smelts	protest
sent	tenth	protect	self	object
fender	sleds	subject	myself	ever

49

Teach word endings /er/, /ing/, /y/, /es/, /s/ and /ed/.

SHORT i

thrifty	impy	frisby	slips	lifting
swiftly	skimpy	flimsy	stilted	sifter
nifty	shrimps	brims	clips	shifting
stinker	chimps	hinting	ships	windy
blinker	blimps	grinch	tipsy	hinder
winking	limping	flinty	fifty	tinder
thinking	Wimpy	glinting	nifty	wispy
slinky	wintry	linty	vista	crispy

---

silky	slinky	sprinter	clinker	figs
milking	tinker	printer	drinking	wins
tilts	bids	minty	gilded	fins
risky	fibs	tinted	spindly	tins
frisky	sits	wilted	dwindling	wits
brisk	bibs	simply	kindling	thins
inky	digs	tilts	crisper	spits
pinker	wigs	jilted	inkling	whimper

---

listing	swishing	lilting	tinkling	sixty
misty	wished	whisker	sprinkling	mixing
sister	dishes	brisker	shrinks	pimply
twisty	fishing	whisper	living	hilt
blister	rigs	disks	giving	inching
fist	dims	filthy	crinkling	sliver
drifting	swims	richer	shiver	filming
drifter	sins	listing	liver	lisping

REVIEW OF THE "SHORT VOWELS"

Teach word endings /er/, /ing/, /y/, /es/, /s/ and /ed/.

SHORT o

romp	frosty	songster	lofty	fondling
stomp	joshing	longing	golfing	fonder
chomped	sloshing	body	shots	Honda
clock	topsy	promptly	spots	ponds
pomp	Flopsy	often	slots	rondo
ponder	dropsy	soften	trots	bonding
lost	proper	bother	plots	cloth
costing	prosper	golfer	clots	froth

---

stronger	stops	socks	fondly	Congo
longer	crops	rocky	blond	yonder
longest	blots	locket	cods	pronto
offers	flops	pocket	of	conch
gongs	globs	docking	onto	poncho
thongs	snobs	shocker	upon	closet
throngs	chops	mocking	off	fronds
songs	shops	rocker	on	gosling

---

frosting	frothy	blocking	gosh	cocky
frost	moths	clocks	slosh	stocky
honking	broth	frocks	posh	foxy
softer	lobster	flocking	galoshes	boxing
crofter	mobster	smocks	drops	agony
lofts	cloth	rocket	props	offer
foster	costing	socket	tops	convent
belongs	throbs	stocking	rocking	content

51

REVIEW OF THE "SHORT VOWELS"

Teach word endings /er/, /ing/, /y/, /es/, /s/ and /ed/.

SHORT u

lumpy	jumbo	crushing	sprung	bumbling
bumpy	stunts	mushy	rung	stumbling
stumps	runty	hush	hung	fumbling
rumps	number	slushy	sung	grumbling
crumpling	slumber	rushed	stung	rumbling
dumpling	hunting	gushing	spuds	tumbling
dusty	punts	plush	funds	plunder
rusty	shunting	slush	brunt	Buster

---

musty	bunting	brushing	grumpy	thumping
crusty	bunts	thrush	crumpet	crunchy
lusty	grunted	bunching	trumpet	lunches
mumps	blunts	brunch	gulping	punched
dumping	luster	gulch	pulpy	plugs
clumper	bluster	mulch	under	thugs
blunder	cluster	such	pumping	struts
lumber	duster	bulk	fungus	slums

---

slugs	just	sulky	thrust	strums
nuts	must	hulks	chunky	trunks
puns	busts	bulbs	bunks	spunky
nuns	gusty	strung	bunking	slumps
bugs	trusty	slung	clunker	husky
clubs	thus	lung	drunk	gulf
cubs	bunch	flung	junking	stub
grubs	hunch	clung	plunking	shuns

52

THE PATTERN OF "ar"

bark	arm	cargo	parchment	start
cart	alarm	pardon	starchy	park
hard	Mars	alarm	scarf	spark
harm	bars	barter	scars	sharp
charm	cars	partner	darling	barb
chart	afar	charming	harmful	arch
harp	jars	starter	sharpener	parch
sharp	par	charter	sparkling	shark

---

part	tar	farther	gargling	Martha
art	army	barman	remarking	harsh
dart	party	carpenter	upstart	marsh
tart	darting	impart	snarling	march
yard	artist	sharpen	garland	smart
card	garden	bartender	garnet	Denmark
lard	charting	apart	garment	remark
hardy	harming	apartment	yardarm	marbling

---

farm	harder	depart	marlin	ensnarl
barn	hardest	department	marmalade	sarcastic
yarn	harken	compartment	harpoon	tarpon
darn	farmer	embark	jargon	varnish
ark	darning	harden	carton	spartan
bark	barking	armrests	cartoon	armful
dark	sharper	hardly	marvel	artistic
lark	sharpest	alarming	parson	stardom

THE PATTERN OF "or"

ford	orbit	morning	sorting	scorch
fort	hornet	shorter	snorting	porch
sort	resort	protector	resort	torch
short	shorter	forest	retort	forth
sport	forbid	torch	color	sort
cork	border	factor	worn	snort
fork	forgot	manor	formal	cork
pork	glory	tornado	factory	corny

_____

port	story	importer	pastor	favor
form	record	florist	normal	reporters
born	razor	corner	instructor	order
storm	inform	unborn	introductory	northern
thorn	reform	corker	inventor	forum
corn	formal	thorny	orders	editor
horn	porker	transform	reforming	organ
morn	forget	shortening	portly	doctor

_____

torn	format	minor	reportedly	ornament
scorn	important	selector	forty	import
shorn	monitor	escalator	forever	export
cord	normal	former	ivory	torment
north	perform	performer	Gordon	humorist
dorm	sporting	shorten	chortling	organizing
York	informal	deform	hornet	lordship
stork	major	elevator	lordly	report
shortly	escorting	resorting	adoring	adornment
informant	orchard	cormorant		

THE PATTERNS OF
"ir"

bird	birth	quirk	smirch
third	girth	skirt	firm
first	mirth	sir	shirt
birch	squirt	dirt	shirk
twirl	squirm	swirl	infirm
girl	whirl	smirk	catbird
stir	Dirk	chirp	astir
fir	flirt	thirsty	confirm

"ur"

burst	purl	turf	burp
curd	furl	surf	blur
curl	hurt	fur	purple
turn	lurch	lurk	blurt
burn	churn	murky	curt
spurn	burl	turkish	spurt
hurl	curb	urn	burnt
church	furnish	slurp	turkey

"er"

perch	perfect	stern	verb
berth	servant	Vern	superb
herb	clerk	alert	filbert
fern	serpent	Bert	insert
serf	perky	pert	lantern
her	herd	western	cavern
herself	person	tavern	superman
jerk	term	sperm	filter

55

THE PATTERNS OF
"oi"

oil	broil	rejoin	anoint
coil	avoid	loin	spoil
spoil	void	point	recoil
foil	tabloid	joint	devoid
tinfoil	coin	appoint	choice
uncoil	join	moist	ointment
boil	groin	hoist	rejoice
toil	enjoin	joist	voice

. . . .

"oy"

boy	employ	soy
cloy	enjoy	troy
coy	envoy	decoy
joy	playboy	destroy
Roy	royal	enjoyment
toy	loyal	employment
ahoy	convoy	royalty
decoy	overjoy	loyalty

. . . .

"ow" as in "now"

brown	how	cowl	flower
clown	now	howl	tower
crown	bow	fowl	bower
down	cow	owl	power
drown	pow	growl	towel
frown	row	jowl	trowel
gown	sow	prowl	vowel
town	vow	yowl	howdy

56

THE PATTERNS OF
"ow" as in "snow"

snow	low	shadow	thrown
blow	bow	widow	flown
crow	show	bowl	growth
grow	slow	lowly	shadowy
now	below	slowly	sown
row	two	blown	disown
stow	glow	own	glowing
flow	window	grown	blowing

. . . .

"ou" as in "out"

out	couch	ground	pout
foul	crouch	bound	dug-out
noun	loud	found	about
ouch	aloud	hound	scout
pouch	cloud	pound	trout
grouch	proud	sound	snout
vouch	shroud	south	spout
slouch	round	mouth	shout

. . . .

THE "ng" SPELLING PATTERNS

"ang"

bang	fang
hang	mustang
clang	rang
sang	tangy
slant	twang
sprang	swang
gang	boomerang

57

THE "ng" SPELLING PATTERNS

"ing"

bring	spring	tinging	morning
cling	string	unstring	opening
ding	swing	coloring	fasting
fling	thing	covering	clinging
king	wing	entering	singing
ling	sling	gathering	mining
ring	sting	gardening	dining
sing	bringing	evening	finding

. . . .

"ong"

long	gong
song	Hong Kong
tong	oblong
strong	prong
along	prolong
among	sarong
belong	thong
ding-dong	throng

. . . .

"ung"

bung	lung
clung	stung
flung	sung
hung	swung
rung	unstrung
slung	unsung
sprung	unhung

COMMON SPELLING PATTERNS

"ck"

pack	jack	beck	sick	slick
back	lack	check	chick	trick
rack	clack	peck	flick	quick
sack	shack	deck	thick	tickling
tack	smack	fleck	sticky	licking
track	snack	neck	stick	ticking
black	stack	reck	kick	slicker
crack	slack	speck	brick	flicker

---

snicker	block	rock	tuck
wicker	cock	mock	truck
pickling	crock	pock	duck
trickling	dock	shock	luck
thicken	frock	smock	cluck
chicken	sock	stock	pluck
stricken	clock	tick-tock	stuck
quicken	lock	padlock	struck

· ·

"ic"

antic	romantic	basic	music	toxic
frantic	hectic	magic	gothic	tunic
plastic	cosmetic	chic	mimic	skeptic
aspic	magnetic	comic	metric	public
spastic	poetic	cosmic	optic	relic
dramatic	athletic	electric	cubic	italic
Slavic	picnic	epic	rustic	arabic

"old"

hold	sold	threshold	fourfold
fold	gold	withold	household
cold	marigold	golden	ninefold
told	scold	behold	stronghold
bold	uphold	blindfold	tenfold
mold	untold	enfold	threefold

. . . .

"ll"

ball	bell	yell	swill
wall	well	shell	thrill
fall	sell	smell	twill
tall	swell	bill	uphill
stall	fell	fill	windmill
call	dwell	kill	refill
mall	jell	skill	frill
recall	spell	still	chill

———————

drill	loll	golly
pill	moll	folly
shrill	dollar	gull
filly	collar	hull
silly	hollow	cull
chilly	follow	skull
hilly	jolly	dull
dill	doll	holly

"ss"

class	pass	less	gloss	hiss
brass	overpass	mess	loss	kiss
bass	underpass	press	moss	amiss
crass	bless	confess	toss	discuss
grass	chess	express	across	Swiss
glass	cress	excess	floss	boss
lass	dress	stress	fuss	cross
mass	profess	unless	cuss	truss

. . . .

"ff"

bluff	scruff	puff	cliff	tiff
buff	gruff	stuff	stiff	chaff
cuff	huff	off	sniff	gaff
ruff	muff	doff	skiff	staff

. . . .

"le"

cable	idle	jumble	grumble	ramble
table	bugle	mumble	temple	scramble
able	dimple	stumble	staple	trample
sable	simple	ample	swindle	kindle
fable	pimple	sample	stifle	single
stable	tumble	nimble	rifle	mingle
gable	crumble	bundle	triple	tingle
noble	fumble	spindle	gamble	spangle
Mable	triangle	angle	people	maple

SIMPLE TWO-SYLLABLE WORDS

Dictate four or five a day

solid	transfer	contrast	forever
until	during	charming	party
music	daring	fever	fifty
habit	format	detect	select
moment	whisper	gravity	itself
carpet	crisper	gravel	within
behind	relax	broken	perfect
belong	invent	superb	reply

---

began	admit	remind	lantern
timber	invest	neglect	intern
secret	trinket	after	hatred
herself	given	morning	acting
himself	chosen	direct	swiftly
demand	prevent	darling	finish
regret	open	expect	anger
embark	even	expand	coldly

---

perhaps	reject	market	father
present	frozen	contract	mother
forget	person	contrast	farther
result	intend	export	brother
pretend	linger	upset	stolen
silent	story	wagon	hundred
golden	study	northern	index
token	duty	western	suspect

continued

remark	resent	driven	permit
inspect	select	driver	insist
credit	tidy	tidbits	inform
prefer	pony	omens	later
subject	protest	reflect	result
exact	insist	simply	limit
partner	number	singly	predict
object	visit	platform	cobweb

---

cabin	prospect	depend	travel
Latin	army	defend	butler
satin	splendid	hotel	ugly
broken	April	motel	finders
taken	forget	depart	spenders

"er" IN TWO-SYLLABLE WORDS

transfer	folder	hinder	alert	over
winter	refer	holder	miser	bumper
butler	fever	anger	fervent	fender
finger	fonder	Peter	serpent	thunder
linger	hamper	infer	convert	paper
never	prefer	rarer	sister	scraper
river	longer	diner	after	stricter
enter	infer	banter	bother	trader

---

super	grinder	filter	modern	permit
banker	planter	crisper	perfect	driver
tanker	perfect	stronger	perform	fixer
member	master	jerking	expert	mixer
monster	mister	canter	perhaps	spender
liver	duster	silver	prosper	joker
broker	refer	bother	shelter	jester
proper	under	safer	singer	jumper

---

number	saver	prefer	stinker	tavern
grander	ever	cavern	dasher	persist
softer	lever	wider	homer	older
sprinter	tamper	hermit	clever	liver
diner	maker	blunder	twister	tinder
closer	simpler	lumber	hanger	lobster
whisper	sampler	finer	printer	superb
stapler	dumper	wafer	jerky	monster
hamster	filter	cluster	quiver	spider

"er" WITH A DOUBLE CONSONANT

differ	manner	spatter	sinner	shopper
offer	teller	slimmer	passer	cropper
supper	speller	wetter	blubber	stopper
dinner	killer	butter	flipper	slipper
butter	filler	beginner	tosser	skidder
stutter	thriller	blotter	spanner	skipper
flutter	kisser	hopper	manner	clipper
summer	shimmer	spotter	bitter	dropper

better	blubber	matter	odder	setter
matter	glimmer	topper	buzzer	scatter
hammer	glitter	tipper	planner	winner
litter	presser	canner	butter	flatter
latter	batter	sputter	bitter	seller
shutter	offer	slimmer	dresser	fatter
runner	dimmer	platter	scrubber	thinner
letter	mutter	rubber	hemmer	flutter

tripper	fitter	ladder	dinner	sinner
jogger	fritter	miller	strummer	swimmer
logger	offer	shipper	buffer	banner
bitter	robber	muffler	whizzer	trimmer
sitter	stiffer	chopper	bigger	bladder
letter	hugger	speller	drummer	adder
chatter	shatter	puffer	coffer	shipper
bobber	slugger	grinner	spinner	fodder

PHONETIC WORDS TO USE IN PRACTISING CONSONANTS AND VOWELS

tablet	control	edit	local	profit
subject	benefit	credit	instruct	finest
bundling	result	outlet	depict	problem
insult	open	inflect	event	focus
habit	contest	direct	depend	basis
visit	prospect	protect	extend	maximum
protect	finest	memo	soda	president
program	begin	product	element	omit

---

rewind	select	adopt	demand	expect
revael	menu	even	elegant	exact
invent	satin	content	lapel	seven
invest	depend	admit	profit	eleven
dining	moment	submit	patron	limit
itself	until	husband	brunch	level
himself	development	stipend	splendid	oldest
hotel	strict	defend	Roman	motel

---

taxing	fact	district	bonus	dumping
result	unit	revolt	distinct	printer
reflect	inspect	index	brand	musical
deduct	respect	constant	moment	respond
proper	insect	apartment	object	complex
catalog	compliment	indirect	seventh	upsets
given	develop	resist	refresh	student
final	pilot	destruct	ninth	sixth

LONG VOWELS

Long vowels are perhaps the most difficult spelling patterns there are. Children are required to learn that more than one letter frequently is used to represent one sound and that there are several patterns that represent each long vowel sound. The old rule, "When two vowels go walking, the first one does the talking," is more wrong than it is right. To present children with such rules is to do the children an injustice because they cannot rely on what they are being taught.

Teach LONG VOWELS as "ways to spell a sound." Teach a long vowel sound to children and then brainstorm for words that contain the sound. Children think of words that contain long a and the teacher records the words on cards. Children may also cut out pictures that represent long a words. These can be placed on a bulletin board with the spelling of the word attached to the picture. Classify the words as to "how the vowel sound is spelled." If you are working with long a...you will find the most common spellings of a-e, ai and ay. In the early grades, practise the most common spelling patterns. As children find other spellings recognize them, list them perhaps but do not practise them. Allow children to generalize from the brainstormed columns. When you say "a" on the end of the word, how will you likely spell it?

Perhaps this is a good time to work with homonyms in your classroom. Many words are spelled differently to reflect different meanings; e.g. pain and pane. Children will enjoy collecting homonyms as they find them in their brainstorming sessions or in their daily writing and reading. The teacher should help children learn the various meanings. Perhaps this is a good time to introduce a simple dictionary to the class.

In the following pages of long vowel dictation, we have added variations

such as ing, ed, es, ce, age and ful. These words should only be dictated
if the children have already been taught these patterns.

"ai"

tail	taint	derail	saint	brain
rail	waif	detail	against	raid
pail	wait	contain	again	aid
sail	flair	restrain	inlaid	paid
fail	air	pertain	disdain	bait
frail	chair	maintain	avail	paint
jail	fair	sustain	unfair	quaint
quail	stair	complain	repair	faint

---

brain	pair	entertain	chairman	retail
chain	hair	retain	mainly	explain
rain	hairy	unpaid	mailman	detain
strain	fairy	postpaid	complaint	remain
stain	diary	repaid	impair	refrain
plain	waist	restraint	exclaim	disdain
pain	claim	unfair	failing	domain
main	aim	repair	sailing	regain

Spain	drain	dispair	prevail	waiter
sprain	snail	airline	brainstorm	obtain
stain	hail	airway	ungainly	container
train	faith	daisy	sustain	aircraft
grain	trail	raisin	remaining	railroad
slain	wail	tailor	unchained	regain
maid	aid	sailor	unclaimed	proclaim
afraid	Craig	trailer	reclaimed	hairless
Gail	laid	flail	gain	trait

brake	hate	pave	pace	invade
bake	plate	stave	space	dedicate
cake	late	brave	race	meditate
lake	rate	engrave	disgrace	demonstrate
flake	crate	forgave	grace	decade
rake	slate	safe	brace	impale
drake	ate	taste	trace	migrate
fake	spade	waste	place	erase

---

lane	trade	age	sale	evade
pale	fade	rage	bale	parade
sale	grade	page	dale	indicate
stale	made	stage	gale	fabricate
scale	wade	wage	male	inflame
James	ape	cage	pale	inflate
tame	grape	gage	tale	unsafe
came	drape	enrage	whale	prepare

---

same	shape	sage	separate	declare
lame	tape	fare	fanfare	became
game	cane	stare	locate	operate
fame	Zane	flare	donate	imitate
dame	Jane	aware	interstate	deflate
blame	pane	snare	beware	eliminate
flame	insane	care	debate	estimate
frame	plane	dare	rotate	escape
shame	make	sake	take	wake

"a-e" continued

grave	spare	elate	cultivate	shave
slave	bare	compare	female	enslave
wave	blare	insane	replace	face
Dave	scare	motivate	nominate	lace
cave	mace	decorate	insulate	excavate
gave	ace	investigate	parkade	elevate

"ay"

pay	Sunday	airway	tray
day	Friday	always	May
say	decay	archway	bray
may	pathway	ashtray	today
lay	relay	betray	belay
Fay	prepay	bluejay	dismay
gay	leeway	byway	inlay
hay	freeway	cutaway	replay

---

jay	interplay	foray	swaying
Kay	display	gangway	sprayed
ray	delay	halfway	grayest
way	crayon	highway	rayon
sway	grayish	holiday	prayer
slay	crayfish	mainstay	stayed
stay	haystack	midway	frayed
spray	payday	Norway	playing

---

stray	overlay	outlay	daresay
clay	payment	outstay	underway
bay	layer	portray	waterway
fray	parlay	railway	workday
gray	maybe	speedway	yesterday
play	astray	subway	byplay
pray	away	underplay	Bombay
quay	player	waylay	Cathay

"ea"

beat	leary	creak	reach	rear
seat	peas	leak	heater	spear
meat	beard	peak	cheater	tear
heat	bean	beak	beater	clear
neat	clean	freak	neater	smear
peat	glean	weak	bleating	weary
feat	jeans	bleak	eastern	dreary
pleat	lean	squeak	nearest	bleary

---

treat	mean	leap	defeat	real
bleat	wean	heap	retreat	steal
wheat	unclean	cheap	dreamer	meal
cheat	cream	sea	creamery	deal
yeast	stream	flea	dealers	heal
beast	dream	reap	shear	peal
feast	team	plea	leaf	seal
least	steam	tea	sheaf	deal

---

east	beam	beneath	teak	cleaner
ear	gleam	underneath	speaker	easing
year	seam	sheath	leaving	greasy
dear	ream	peach	weaving	reason
fear	read	preach	reveal	treason
gear	bead	teach	preacher	season
hear	lead	beach	meanest	defeat
near	plead	each	featuring	mistreat
yearling	cheaper	cleaner	neater	zeal

"ee"

bee	feet	degree	banshee	sleep
tree	beet	meek	carefree	sheep
see	meet	tweet	chimpanzee	steep
fee	seep	sweet	disagree	deep
free	sheet	freezing	employee	weep
glee	sleet	sneezing	forsee	sweep
flee	greet	cheering	pioneer	keep
agree	creep	greeting	velveteen	peep

---

need	reef	steer	Galilee	peer
weed	beef	cheeky	garnishee	veer
deed	jeep	deer	goatee	sneer
feed	street	agreement	grandee	screech
freed	seen	keeper	jamboree	teepee
heed	queen	keeping	jubilee	esteem
seed	teen	sleeping	oversee	discreet
steed	been	teeth	referee	speech

---

speed	green	between	hayseed	eel
bleed	sheen	week	linseed	feel
creed	fleet	peek	cogwheel	creel
tweed	beer	seek	redeem	peel
greed	steer	sleek	sixteen	steel
breed	queer	creek	fifteen	cheek
eel	sheer	leeks	unseen	asleep
feel	cheer	reek	umpteen	sweeper
wintergreen	career	musketeer	rootbeer	veneer

these	grebe	adhere	Swede
here	eke	ampere	sincere
sere	theme	cashmere	insincere
eve	convene	inhere	Chinese
Steve	gangrene	interfere	Japanese
mede	serene	Paul Revere	Cantonese
mere	intervene	persevere	Maltese
were	Nazarene	severe	Portugese

---

athlete	replete
compete	secrete
complete	extreme
concrete	impede
delete	stampede
deplete	evening
incomplete	Pete
Siamese	obsolete

"ie"

shriek	belief	mischief	movie
shiek	relief	unbelief	sharpie
field	brief	priest	rookie
shield	chief	handkerchief	cookie
windshield	grief	fierce	Dixie
yield	kerchief	pierce	believe
infield	thief	lassie	achieve
afield	relief	Lorie	grieve

---

relieve	ponies	duties
reprieve	rubies	Indies
thieve	pigmies	economies
retrieve	remedies	fairies
disbelieve	series	fisheries
cavities	parties	miseries
charities	reveries	pansies
comedies	nineties	peonies

"i-e"

ride	bribe	tile	quite	pine
glide	tribe	kite	despite	spine
stride	pride	bite	invite	vine
hide	side	smite	alike	gripe
bride	jibe	spite	desire	ripe
slide	dive	sprite	unite	stripe
tide	drive	rise	entire	snipe
wide	five	wise	provide	pipe

---

time	alive	dire	astride	strike
dime	hive	fire	reside	file
grime	chives	afire	divide	mile
chime	thrive	hire	yuletide	Nile
lime	rife	desire	empire	pile
slime	wives	tire	incline	vile
mime	wife	wire	inside	wiles
prime	life	vampire	arise	bile

---

brine	spike	wipe	bedside	feline
dine	unlike	swipe	besides	porcupine
fine	hike	tripe	combine	valentine
shine	bike	entire	define	iodine
thine	dike	lined	refine	shoreline
line	like	excite	quite	bagpipes
mine	Mike	mobile	describe	wise
nine	pike	size	aspire	devise
arise	despise	merchandise	inspire	reside

77

"igh"

high	slight	sighing	sprightly
sigh	bright	lighting	rightly
sight	right	brighter	brightly
tight	fright	fighting	foresight
might	plight	frighten	lightning
fight	flight	mighty	twilight
light	blight	tighten	lighten
night	Dwight	slightly	delight

---

thigh	insight	airtight
brighten	limelight	goodnight
nigh	skylight	aright
frightening	overnight	candlelight
highest	moonlight	midnight
sunlight	outright	downright
copyright	sidelight	footlight
higher	tonight	spotlight

"ie"

die	vies	amplified	justified
pie	flies	complied	pried
lie	cries	defied	purified
magpie	fireflies	denied	stupified
necktie	fortifies	died	satisfied
ties	plies	dried	tied
lies	supplies	lied	spied
untie	tries	implied	mortified

---

petrified

gratifies

intensified

multiplied

purified

relied

replied

sanctified

"o-e"

vote	lore	wove	arose	stone
note	sore	globe	expose	more
rote	chore	robe	impose	bore
dote	wore	hole	enclose	core
tote	quote	pole	dispose	store
code	crone	mole	disclose	shore
rode	tone	sole	zone	pore
cone	drone	stole	ozone	fore

_____

bone	hose	galore	remote	froze
hone	chose	explore	erode	Rome
those	nose	repose	smote	strove
throne	pose	abode	strobe	cove
quote	rose	spoke	parole	cloves
choke	close	gore	explode	grove
broke	home	snore	deplore	rove
smoke	dome	adore	invoke	stove

_____

joke	tore	remote	microbe	denote
alone	rope	scone	wardrobe	devote
lone	cope	stoke	episode	decode
stroke	dope	implore	forebode	promote
woke	hope	before	postpone	ashore
yoke	lope	restore	sunstroke	ignore
shone	slope	awoke	bloke	propose
prone	mope	provoke	console	repose
tadpole	elope	backbone	limestone	telescope

coat	afloat	overboard	load
boat	soap	outboard	toad
bloat	roam	inboard	foam
float	loam	starboard	loam
goat	oath	oats	coal
throat	oar	pasteboard	foal
moat	soar	shuffleboard	goal
gloat	road	inroad	shoal

———————————

boast	aboard	oaths	boar
roast	board	gloaming	shipboard
toast	coach	roaming	cupboard
coast	poach	uproar	blackboard
Joan	roach	roam	dashboard
loan	afloat	seafoam	abroad
moan	foamy	coaches	hoard
groan	soapy	poaches	switchboard

———————————

oak	gloat	charcoal	lifeboat
soak	gunboat	motorboat	steamboat
cloak	overcoat	buckboard	cutthroat
croak	rowboat	cardboard	loaves
oaf	sailboat	clapboard	moaning
loaf	speedboat	redcoat	groaning
road	topcoat	billboard	floater
goad	waistcoat	scapegoat	coasting

bow	bowl	slow	grown
blow	lowly	know	thrown
flow	narrow	snow	shown
grow	slowly	row	overthrown
show	blown	tow	follow
crow	own	stow	gallows
glow	disown	below	overgrown
low	flown	growing	grown

---

snowy	window	slowest	pillow
snowing	widow	rowing	willow
blower	overflow	crows	billow
glowing	shadow	towing	elbow
lower	rainbow	towrope	aglow
lowest	roadshow	yellow	growth
shows	scarecrow	mellow	overgrowth
slower	sorrow	fellow	shadowy

"old"

old	hold	untold	blindfold
told	scold	resold	foothold
mold	golden	scolding	foretold
fold	holding	tenfold	manifold
gold	folded	behold	uphold
sold	olden	marigold	withhold
bold	colder	stronghold	folder
cold	retold	threshhold	household

"olt"

bolt	bolted
colt	molting
dolt	colts
jolt	jolted
molt	thunderbolt
volt	bolting
revolt	molted
voltage	volts

"u-e"

sure	future	dilute	misrule	brute
fluke	manure	excuse	ridicule	fume
duke	exude	confuse	vestibule	prude
huge	compute	transfuse	profuse	prune
June	extrude	refuse	reuse	mute
tune	impure	peruse	impute	dude
rule	consume	repute	delude	spruce
mule	insure	refute	Neptune	truce

---

cure	include	resolute	rebuke	dispute
lure	seclude	absolute	disuse	institute
dune	conclude	ruse	parachute	constitute
tube	interlude	figure	creature	tribute
lube	prelude	secure	feature	chute
Rube	intrude	picture	enclosure	astute
cube	abuse	nature	introduce	salute
pure	amuse	endure	reduce	execute

---

jute	crude	exposure	induce	endure
cute	plume	manicure	deduce	denude
use	resume	mature	produce	nurture
fuse	volume	pasture	exclude	injure
yule	tribune	scripture	deluge	procure
flute	perfume	lecture	refute	insecure
nude	costume	posture	spume	adventure
rude	refuse	demure	persecute	expenditure

84

GRADE THREE DICTATION

Review 1-1 Relationships Sequence

and

Add Common Patterns

"er"

faster	monster	Chester	hinder
master	softer	sprinter	disaster
plaster	fonder	smelter	remember
planter	yonder	shelter	October
hamper	ponder	under	September
camper	longer	timber	November
rafter	stronger		suspender
pamper			forever

_____

spender	bluster	tiger	hover
fender	duster	Peter	consider
blender	hunter	anger	bewilder
lender	lumber	proper	paper
tender	jumper	temper	defender
jester	cluster	butler	deliver
fester	bumper	linger	prisoner
helper	bunter	slender	timber

_____

blister	splinter	ever	together
sister	ember	amber	beholder
mister	tinder	gander	carpenter
winter	sander	finger	publisher

"er" continued

hinder	banter	winter	sandpaper
tinder	Denver	printer	performer
drifter	silver	pelter	sprinter
planter	number	softer	drifter
finger	super	whisper	fixer

handy	dusty	wiry	foolishly	frosty
candy	crusty	only	perfectly	fondly
sandy	grumpy	scanty	enemy	softly
crafty	lumpy	spunky	permanently	costly
dandy	jumpy	flunky	importantly	Monty
hanky	rusty	frisky	lucky	body
shanty	bumpy	corny	yucky	lofty
nasty	gusty	thorny	gucky	sloppy

---

hefty	sleepy	ornery	plucky	salty
zesty	dusty	stormy	fluffy	springy
plenty	baby	forty	stuffy	tingly
twenty	Tony	seventy	puppy	tenderly
pesty	spindly	tasty	guppy	trusty
pesky	trimly	pastry	stubby	flashy
lefty	kindly	scary	chubby	crunchy
Wendy	wildly	Mary	tubby	strongly

---

nifty	blindly	orderly	holly	identity
windy	sulky	properly	folly	humanity
stinky	sultry	property	Molly	distinctly
misty	simply	ability	dolly	responsibility
fifty	tiny	activity	Polly	probably
sixty	empty	stupidly	spotty	directly
twisty	zany	elderly	bossy	secondly
slinky	wintry	exactly	mossy	family
silly	Billy	chilly	muddy	jelly

"ing"

cramping	jumping	spitting	depending	frosting
camping	rushing	fitting	selecting	chomping
stamping	flushing	kissing	reflecting	prompting
landing	bumping	dipping	restricting	costing
handing	grumbling	missing	stretching	bonding
strangling	hunting	hissing	representing	romping
lasting	blushing	dripping	dividing	stomping
tangling	dusting	gripping	revolving	choking

---

bending	splashing	spotting	publishing	shedding
resting	smashing	stopping	abandoning	bedding
tending	flashing	trotting	thundering	wetting
nesting	crashing	flopping	contacting	getting
cresting	thrashing	shopping	trucking	letting
trembling	slashing	hopping	clucking	humming
jesting	itching	crossing	chucking	hemming
testing	stitching	tossing	plucking	betting

---

limping	wishing	strumming	starching	muttering
sifting	fishing	drumming	scorching	fluttering
swinging	tapping	slugging	blanching	littering
hinting	slapping	stuffing	lunching	flittering
thinking	spelling	lurching	munching	puttering
drinking	dwelling	tugging	crunching	chattering
lifting	pressing	puffing	perching	directing
twisting	dressing	sputtering	pinching	exacting
probing	perfecting	considering	delivering	plastering

88

PHONETIC WORDS

basket	combat	filmstrip	demon
disgust	total	candid	diving
vitamin	limpet	camera	extend
consult	respond	depth	expand
salad	bacon	talent	intend
consist	hamlet	crimson	resting
vital	elect	arisen	sunset
compact	behind	napkin	silent

---

trumpet	conflict	disposal	impact
tuna	constant	potent	signal
halibut	rental	detest	stop
criminal	casket	panel	drifting
instant	suspect	marigold	inching
dental	focus	untold	enchant
Spanish	distract	behold	pumpkin
tomato	spoken	dragon	human

Mexican	evil	wagon	robin
cupid	taken	bantam	panel
distant	golden	stimulus	including
defendant	zero	defrost	wisest
dependent	reprimand	distrust	French
devil	remind	mistrust	swiftest
contradict	rascal	distend	canvas
tempt	trident	tempest	slanting

Phonetic Words continued

lunch	undid	bathtub	dishpan
stupid	present	lemon	reset
insult	upon	Simon	instep
animal	latest	beyond	unplug
token	transact	cactus	asking
contempt	extinct	living	utmost
fifth	establish	hiding	widen
Bingo	polish	frozen	unjust

---

twelfth	benefit	widest	handling
diet	suet	branching	acting
refreshment	document	sandbox	admit
tenth	contract	regret	unsold

"er" Practice for "Good Spellers"

personal	distemper	deserver	filtering
understand	converter	terminus	helicopter
universal	deliver	fervent	everything
sternly	publisher	eraser	servant
informer	jetliner	advertisement	impersonate
confer	discover	dismember	fingertip
consider	properly	misery	deserving
fingertip	computer	lateral	whispering

---

recover	consumer	fertilizer	Bernard
camera	hanger	examiner	another
Alexander	funeral	polisher	deserting
interpret	anger	hovering	Roberta
remember	hunger	superman	perfectly
government	vertical	reserving	trumpeter
interest	minerals	interesting	fluster
perfect	perfectly	preserver	recover

---

superb	disaster	cluster	bluster
herself	reminder	modern	deserving
property	defender	fermenting	tenderizing
adviser	whenever	persistent	ruler
verdict	conserver	informer	finisher
opener	imperfect	blistering	fisherman
every	foster	sampler	entering
traveler	alabaster	hindering	tolerant

"er" words   continued

dispenser	condenser	imperfect	serpent
permanent	carpenter	northern	smoldering
sandpaper	terminal	westerly	lantern
September	cucumber	tinkering	afternoon
defender	everlasting	federal	midterm
October	forever	customer	inserting
November	impertinent	gathering	plastering
suspender	eternal	together	altering

fabric	antic	microscopic	optic
tonic	aspic	ironic	tropic
plastic	spastic	supersonic	economic
public	anemic	bubonic	music
dramatic	politic	harmonic	titanic
antagonistic	prolific	melodic	majestic
drastic	static	sardonic	artistic
electric	rustic	Nordic	colic

---

frantic	caloric	capitalistic	panoramic
cosmic	republic	electronic	monastic
cosmetic	astronomic	antiseptic	heraldic
fantastic	democratic	ethnic	futuristic
historic	mimic	gothic	satanic
bionic	gigantic	humanistic	Hispanic
topic	panic	diagnostic	Pacific
Atlantic	metric	animalistic	Arabic

Arithmetic	organic	statistic	Baltic
athletic	heroic	Panasonic	Slavic
platonic	moronic	balistic	traffic
sonic	hectic	coptic	attic
prolific	acoustic	poetic	comic
sporadic	dietetic	stoic	prosaic
fanatic	elastic	masonic	septic

Change "y" to "i" - Add "es" or "ed"

duty	pigmy	cavity	bunny
duties	pigmies	cavities	bunnies
fairy	forty	ninety	candy
fairies	forties	nineties	candies
lily	twenty	pansy	empty
lilies	twenties	pansies	emptied
ruby	pony	remedy	entry
rubies	ponies	remedies	entries

---

study	mutiny	try	amplify
studied	mutinied	tries	amplifies
marry	vary	tried	implied
married	varied	dry	denies
weary	palsy	dries	spies
wearied	palsied	dried	fried
candy	curtsy	replies	justifies
candied	curtsied	replied	satisfied

. . . .

Add "d"

blame	convene	bribe	handle
blamed	convened	bribed	handled
time	drone	name	rumble
timed	droned	named	rumbled
choke	rule	cure	cable
choked	ruled	cured	cabled
tune	crane	revere	title
tuned	craned	revered	titled

94

hope	stampede	cube
hoped	stampeded	cubed
interfere	enthrone	fire
interfered	enthroned	fired
shape	bottle	elope
shaped	bottled	eloped
hike	use	graze
hiked	used	grazed
smile	compete	pile
smiled	competed	piled

· ·

Add "ed"

stamp	rust	plaster	wilt
stamped	rusted	plastered	wilted
dump	act	enter	cheat
dumped	acted	entered	cheated
blast	shunt	fluster	frost
blasted	shunted	flustered	frosted
chant	heat	hinder	crest
chanted	heated	hindered	crested

———————

branded	exited	ended	landed
enacted	bumped	hampered	romped
hunted	cramped	thumped	blended
tramped	limped	festered	locked

Double Consonant Before Adding "ed"

flap	sip	flip	skimmed	fretted
flapped	sipped	flipped	netted	whizzed
hop	hum	grin	mugged	penned
hopped	hummed	grinned	flitted	strutted
sup	cram	chop	ragged	spotted
supped	crammed	chopped	pinned	planned

· ·

Short oo

wood	goody	hook	toot	outlook
good	woody	took	uproot	pothook
hood	roof	look	tooth	undertook
stood	spoof	crook	booth	unhook
understood	aloof	nook	shoot	textbook
dogwood	waterproof	shook	flatfoot	
driftwood	book	afoot	uproot	
motherhood	brook	scoot	mistook	

· ·

Long oo

soon	brood	spool	mushroom	lagoon
bloom	food	tool	taproom	crooner
shampoo	mood	coon	cartoon	boost
bamboo	broody	croon	baboon	stoop
igloo	cool	moon	macaroon	trooping
kangaroo	stool	broom	teaspoon	nincompoop
bazoo	pool	zoom	saloon	droopy
skidoo	drool	groom	dragoon	pontoon

"able"

table	capable	pardonable
stable	disable	usable
fable	enable	teachable
able	durable	seasonable
gable	likeable	probable
cable	lovable	readable
sable	passable	printable
time table	portable	unstable

---

desirable	incapable	constable
adorable	improbable	detachable
delectable	incomparable	deplorable
reasonable	navigable	escapable
punishable	perishable	explicable
presentable	notable	valuable
personable	indispensable	removable
vegetable	formidable	unavoidable

"tion"

notion	vacation	reservation	tradition
lotion	devotion	inflation	navigation
potion	promotion	imitation	motivation
nation	condition	nutrition	sensation
station	invitation	estimation	rotation
ration	donation	implication	graduation
motion	isolation	position	formation
emotion	petition	fumigation	tuition

---

meditation	competition	civilization	negation
lubrication	obligation	duration	elimination
preservation	admiration	edition	locomotion
disposition	destination	calculation	jubilation
superstition	condition	malnutrition	condensation
recognition	mutation	fashion	salvation
substation	stimulation	hesitation	ignition
temptation	transportation	revelation	position

---

presentation	impersonation	recognition	observation
composition	petition	eradication	identification
fixation	quotation	fortification	repetition
reduction	reputation	composition	ambition
caution	speculation	premonition	vibration
prohibition	tabulation	vexation	probation
exposition	induction	organization	publication
salutation	vocation	partition	notation

"all"

hall	befall	overall	waterfall
ball	catcall	pitfall	squall
call	Cornwall	rainfall	basketball
fall	downfall	recall	baseball
mall	eyeball	windfall	bookstall
tall	footfall	stall	forestall
wall	install	thrall	enthrall
all	nightfall	small	

"re"

redo	refrain	remake	replant
remember	reproduce	restate	resent
remain	refried	retell	relent
reuse	reconsider	reclaim	recoil
reread	replay	repeat	retold
repaint	retain	rebuilt	reconsider
rewrite	reform	repent	refit
reenter	retake	restart	resell

"dis"

dislike	dispell	disrupt	discard
dismiss	disturb	dismember	discontent
disappear	dismantle	disjointed	distaste
distinct	disgrace	dissent	disconnect
disfigure	distinct	disbelief	disclaim
disappoint	disdain	discord	display
dismay	distance	disprove	dispend

"un"

unfit	underdog	ungrateful	uncorked
until	untold	unfriendly	undesirable
unwise	unstick	undercover	unprinted
unable	unsold	undermined	unspent
under	unpleasant	underpaid	unspeakable
unpick	unfold	unthinking	undependable
uncover	uncooked	unattend	uninformed
unbend	unchained	unpublished	unanswered

"uni"

unit	united	union
unison	university	reunion
universe	community	unionist
unicorn	universal	unify
uniform	unity	uniformity
unilateral	unicycle	unified
unite	immunity	unification
reunite	communion	uniflow

"bi"

bicycle	bicorn
biform	bible
bivalve	bifocal
biceps	biology
bilateral	bipod
biplane	bipolar
binocular	bisect
bicuspid	biography

"tri"

tricycle	triad
tripod	triangle
triple	tricolor
trident	trinity
trillium	trio
tribunal	triplicate
triplets	triceps
trivet	tribunal

"be"

between	before	begone	beneath
beyond	become	befriend	because
beside	berate	bespoken	behold
below	beware	beginning	belittle
behave	became	betrothed	believe
beget	befall	behind	befuddle
betwixt	belong	beset	bestow
beloved	bedeck	beseech	betoken

. . . .

"sub"

subway	substandard	submarine
sublet	sublime	substitute
subsist	subsidy	subordinate
subtropical	subdivide	subnormal
subtract	subalpine	subcontract
submit	subarctic	subserve
subplot	suborbital	subscribe
subject	submerge	suburb

. . . .

"super"

superb	superman	superclass
supersafe	superhuman	superimpose
supercargo	supermarket	supernatural
supernal	superclass	superpower
superfine	superheat	supervalue
superintend	supersonic	superficial
superior	superstitious	superintendent
superstructure	supervise	supervisor

"auto"

automat	automobile
automatic	automotive
autocrat	autocade
autocratic	autonomy
autoharp	automower
autobus	autocamp
autocab	autobiography
autophone	autograph